A GIFT FOR

_____

FROM

_____

PAR FOR THE COURSE
Design copyright © 2007 by Hallmark Licensing, Inc.
Text copyright © by Steve Riach and VisionQuest
Communications Group Inc.

Published by Hallmark Books, a division of Hallmark Cards, Inc.,
Kansas City, MO 64141.
Visit us on the Web at www.Hallmark.com.

Editorial Director: Todd Hafer
Art Director: Kevin Swanson
Production Artist: Dan C. Horton
Designer: Craig Bissell

ISBN: 978-1-59530-177-2

BOK2077

Printed and bound in China

PAR
FOR THE
COURSE

GOLF TIPS & QUIPS
STATS & STORIES

BY
STEVE
RIACH

ACKNOWLEDGEMENTS

This book is the result of months of research and documentation. As with projects of this magnitude, I received much help from many caring people. I would like to thank the following:

My wonderful wife and children, who gave me their constant love and support, and often unselfishly sacrificed in order to allow me the necessary quiet time to write this book.

My mother, who always inspired me to dream, and continues to do so.

My research aide for this book, Nelson Staats, who once again did a wonderful job in the numerous hours he spent researching facts and chasing down information.

My good friend Dr. Lance Rawlings, with whom I seem to be forever trading stories like those found in this book and laughing like kids at the memories of some of these moments.

The Board of Directors of the Heart of a Champion Foundation, for their commitment to seeing sports stories used to help shape character in young people all across America.

And Todd Hafer at Hallmark, who believed in this book and was responsible for it becoming a reality.

Finally, I dedicate this book to the memory of my father, Tom Riach, who passed from this life on October 6, 2006. He loved to play the game of golf and enjoyed the many personalities of the game. More than that, he loved to spend a day on the course with his son – often spending more time helping me look for lost balls off the course than actually playing his own shots on the course – an exercise I truly looked forward to. Many of my fondest memories of time spent with my dad are from those days together on golf courses in California, Virginia, Arizona, and Texas. The real connection to the game for me certainly came through those times. I will miss my father as my occasional golf partner, yet much more so as my dad.

Golf is best when enjoyed with the people you care about. I hope this book provides enjoyment for you and those you love, just as playing the game did for me and my dad.

ABOUT THE AUTHOR

Steve Riach is a principal and founder of SER Media and the president and co-founder of VisionQuest Communications Group, Inc., two Dallas-based media companies. He is an award-winning producer, writer, and director of numerous television, film, and video projects, and is one of the nation's foremost creators of virtue-based and positive-themed sports content. Steve's programs have been seen on ESPN, FOX Sports, NBC, and a variety of broadcast and cable television outlets. He is also the principal behind the creative vision for the *Heart of a Champion*® brand of sports-related programs and properties. His start in sports media came as an on-air personality, hosting national television and radio programming.

A prolific writer, Steve has authored *Passion for the Game, Above the Rim, The Drive to Win, Inspire a Dream, It's How You Play the Game, Life Lessons from Auto Racing, Life Lessons from Golf, Life Lessons from Baseball, Heart of a Champion: Profiles in Character,* and *Amazing But True Sports Stories* and *Amazing Athletes, Amazing Moments.*

Steve is also the co-founder of the *Heart of a Champion Foundation*, a non-profit organization devoted to producing materials designed to teach character and virtue to children. Steve is creator and author of the foundation's *Heart of a Champion® Character Development Program*, a leading tool for the character development/education of students in schools across America.

A former college baseball player at the University of the Pacific, Steve is also a frequent speaker to school groups, youth agencies, corporations, sports organizations, and churches.

Steve Riach

HEART OF A CHAMPION

The *Heart of a Champion Foundation* is an independent, national non-profit organization using the platform of sports to build and reinforce character and virtue in young people. Blending the message and the messenger, the Heart of a Champion Foundation's winning formula teaches and models character education at the grassroots level, to mold better citizens and develop the heart of a champion in youth.

The *Heart of a Champion*® school program is an in-class character education program that teaches positive values through video, audio, and written vignettes featuring popular and respected athletes and other role models. Teaching virtues through "sight-and-sound" stories of positive role models attracts the attention of learners and arouses their interest, raising questions that lead to discussions and reflections about implementing those virtues into daily life. Stories that demonstrate values such as honesty, perseverance, courage, commitment, discipline, integrity, and fairness encourage students to recognize and follow their examples. The Heart of a Champion program also includes student, teacher, and parent enrichment materials to reinforce the positive character traits that are taught and discussed. The Heart of a Champion Foundation believes that training young people in character and virtue can build champions for tomorrow through stories of the heroes of today. For more information, visit the Web site at www.heartofachampion.org or call (817) 427-4621.

Heart of a Champion® is a registered trademark under which virtuous sports products and programs are created and distributed. Materials include award-winning videos, television and radio programs, films, books, and Internet activities.

OFF THE TEE

GREAT GOLF TRIVIA

DID YOU KNOW?

During the reign of Caesar, the Romans
played a game resembling golf by striking
a feather-stuffed ball with club-shaped
tree branches.

The Dutch played a similar game on
their frozen canals circa the 15th century.

In 1457, golf was banned in Scotland because
it interfered with the practice of archery,
which was crucial to the country's military defense.
Nevertheless, the Scots continued to brave the
opposition of both Parliament and church by
playing the game on seaside courses called links.

Scotland boasts the world's oldest golf course,
St. Andrews, used as early as the 16th century.

In the 1800s, the gutta-percha ball ("gutty")
replaced the traditional feather-filled ball.

In 1860, the first British Open was played
at Prestwick, Scotland.

The first 18-hole course in the U.S.,
the Chicago Golf Club, was founded near
Wheaton, IL, in 1893.

International golf competition dates from 1922,
when teams of American and British amateurs
first competed for the Walker Cup. Five years
later, the Ryder Cup series between professionals
of the two nations was launched.

In 1919, Walter Hagen became the first
full-time tournament pro.

The National Golf Foundation estimates there
are more than 26 million golfers in the U.S.

Each year, U.S. golfers spend nearly
600 million dollars on equipment.

A maximum of 14 clubs may be used in
tournament play.

U.S. golf balls must be at least 1.68 inches in
diameter and weigh no more than 1.62 ounces.

IN 1988, CURTIS STRANGE

BECAME THE FIRST

MILLION-DOLLAR-A-YEAR

PLAYER.

Golf courses and practice facilities in the U.S.
number about 15,000.

Between 1923 and 1930, Bobby Jones
won five U.S. Amateurs, four U.S. Opens,
three British Opens, and one British Amateur.
His four memorable victories in 1930 gave
him an unprecedented Grand Slam.

In 1971, Jack Nicklaus became the first golfer
to win more than $200,000 in a single season.
He also was the first to earn more than
$300,000 (in 1972).

In 1968, Arnold Palmer was the first golfer to
pass the million-dollar mark in career earnings.

In 1988, Nicklaus, the only golfer to be chosen
five times as the PGA Player of the Year,
became the first player to earn more than
$5 million in a career.

South African golfer Gary Player is the winner
of most major events worldwide — three
British Opens, three Masters, two PGA titles,
and one U.S. Open.

Sam Snead won a record 84 PGA tournaments.

On April 13, 1986, 46-year-old Jack Nicklaus
became the oldest player to win the Masters.
In 1997, Tiger Woods, at 21 years 3 months
and 14 days, became the youngest
Masters winner.

Ben Hogan was the first to win three major tournaments in one year. In 1953, he won the Masters, the U.S. Open, and the British Open.

Jack Nicklaus went 17 straight years with at least one PGA Tour win ('62-'78).

Byron Nelson went 113 straight tournaments in the 1940s, never missing a cut along the way.

Sam Snead holds the record for most career PGA Tour wins with 81. The only major tournament he never won was the U.S. Open.

Sam Snead also holds the PGA record for
most wins at a single event, winning the
Greater Greensboro Open eight times.

Phil Mickelson is the only lefty to win the
U.S. Amateur event (1990).

The leading money winner on the men's
golf tour in 1936 was Horton Smith.
He earned $7,682.

Hale Irwin was a two-time All Big Eight
defensive back at the University of Colorado.

ESTEBAN TOLEDO HAD

A 12-1 RECORD AS A

PRO BOXER FIGHTING

OUT OF THE

LIGHTWEIGHT DIVISION.

Fred Funk was the golf coach at the University
of Maryland from 1982 to 1988.

The 1954 U.S. Open champion, Ed Furgol,
overcame a childhood accident that resulted in his
left arm being six inches shorter than his right.

In winning the 1968 PGA Championship at
age 48, Julius Boros became the oldest man
to win a major tournament.

Greg Norman's infamous final-round meltdown at the 1996 Masters occurred on April 14, which is the anniversary of two notable tragedies: the assassination of Abraham Lincoln in 1865 and the sinking of the Titanic in 1912.

The only man ever to play in a Masters tournament and a baseball World Series was Sam Byrd, who played in the 1931 World Series with the New York Yankees and had top-five finishes at the Masters in 1941 and 1942.

Jack McGurn, a competing amateur at the 1933 Western Open, was arrested during the second round of play when it was learned he was "Machine Gun Jack," the notorious hit man for Al Capone.

LPGA cofounder Patty Berg once quarterbacked a youth football team that included future football coaching legend Bud Wilkinson.

The great Bobby Jones was just 28 years old when he retired from competitive golf in 1930. Jones held college degrees in English literature, engineering, and law.

At the 1998 Solheim Cup, American Tammie
Green played while six months pregnant.

In 1954, the USGA gave a special gift to then
President Eisenhower — a putting green on the
south lawn of the White House.

Chi Chi Rodriguez was a teammate of future
baseball Hall of Famer Roberto Clemente while
playing on a Class A minor league team in
Puerto Rico in 1953.

In 1985, German Bernhard Langer became the
first golfer ever to earn his first professional tour
victory in the U.S. at the Masters.

IN 1974, SAM SNEAD
FINISHED THIRD AT
THE PGA CHAMPIONSHIP
AND SECOND AT THE
LOS ANGELES OPEN —
NO ORDINARY FEAT
CONSIDERING SNEAD
WAS 62 AT THE TIME.

Sportswriter Grantland Rice coined the term
Amen Corner for the three-hole stretch on
Augusta National's back nine.

Jerry Pate won the 1976 U.S. Open
in his first event after turning pro.

1945 was a historic year for Byron Nelson.
Most golf fans know that "Lord Byron"
won a record 11 consecutive tournaments
in what became the most amazing streak in
the history of the sport. What is sometimes lost
in celebration of the streak is the fact that
Nelson captured a record total of
18 tournaments that year.

In 1980, Dave Eichelberger won the Bay Hill Classic while wearing women's panty hose to help ward off the wind and cold.

The maiden name of Barbara Nicklaus, wife of golf legend Jack Nicklaus, is Barbara Bush.

The top tax-payer in all of Shenzhen, China, in 2001 was none other than Tiger Woods. Woods paid $4.2 million yuan (about $500,000) in taxes on his undisclosed appearance fee during a promotional tournament. News about Woods paying more in taxes than anyone in the People's Republic of China — a country of 1.3 billion people — spread fast and made headlines all over the world. Woods found the news somewhat amusing. "That's actually pretty funny," Woods said. "But it's not that funny."

Woodrow Wilson was known as the most avid golfer of any U.S. President. He was known to play six rounds of golf in a given week — in any type of weather. In winter, he used red golf balls so he could find them in the snow. His caddie was required to carry a flashlight for rounds played in the evening. He once played a match that did not end until 5 a.m.

For the movie *Tin Cup*, it took actor Kevin Costner 86 takes to hit the shot that he banks off the portable toilet and onto the green, rolling right up to the camera lens. The scene took nearly the entire day to film and lasted just 10 seconds on the screen.

THEY
SAID
IT

NOTABLE GOLF QUOTES

GOLF IS...

"Golf is a game whose aim is to hit a very small
ball into an even smaller hole, with weapons
singularly ill-designed for the purpose."

WINSTON CHURCHILL

"Golf is an awkward set of bodily contortions
designed to produce a graceful result."

TOMMY ARMOUR

"Golf is neither a microcosm of nor a
metaphor for life. It is a sport, bloodless sport,
if you don't count ulcers."

DICK SCHAAP

"Golf is much more fun than walking naked
in a strange place, but not much."

BUDDY HACKETT

"Golf is an expensive way of playing marbles."

G.K. CHESTERTON

"They say that life is a lot like golf – don't
believe them. Golf is a lot more complicated."

GARDNER DICKINSON

"Golf is 90 percent inspiration
and 10 percent perspiration."

JOHNNY MILLER

"Golf is the hardest game in the world.
There's no way you can ever get it. Just when
you think you do, the game jumps up
and puts you in your place."

BEN CRENSHAW

"Golf is a game where the ball always lies
poorly and the player lies well."

ANONYMOUS

"Golf is like solitaire. When you cheat,
you cheat only yourself."

TONY LEMA

"Golf is a game in which you yell fore,
shoot six, and write down five."

PAUL HARVEY

"Golf is a game of inches. The most important
are those between the ears."

ARNOLD PALMER

"Golf is so popular simply because it is the best game in the world in which to be bad."

A.A. MILNE, CREATOR OF WINNIE THE POOH

"Golf is a test of temper, a trial of honor, a revealer of character."

DAVID FORGAN

"Golf is not a game of great shots. It's a game of the most accurate misses. The people who win make the smallest mistakes."

GENE LITTLER

"GOLF IS LIKE CHASING

A QUININE PILL AROUND A

COW PASTURE."

WINSTON CHURCHILL

"Golf is a puzzle without an answer.
I've played the game for 40 years, and I still
haven't the slightest idea how to play."

GARY PLAYER

"It's probably the best sport man has invented,
because you never conquer it, and because of
the beauty of the surroundings. Every shot is
different. Every hole is different. For some
idiotic reason, we all like the challenge."

CHARLES SCHULZ

"Golf is a good walk spoiled."

MARK TWAIN

GOLF PHILOSOPHY

"Never be a hero when you don't have to be.
Play for the scorecard, not your ego."

JACK NICKLAUS

"I couldn't tell you what exactly I like
about golf. Just when you think you've got it
mastered, it lets you know that you haven't.
I'm just crazy enough to do it."

CLINT EASTWOOD

"Competitive golf is played mainly
on a five-and-a-half inch course:
the space between your ears."

BOBBY JONES

"The game of golf is not how many good shots
you hit. It's how few bad shots you hit."

JACK NICKLAUS

"The golfer has more enemies than any other
athlete. He has 14 clubs in his bag, all of them
different; 18 holes to play; and all around him
are sand, trecs, grass, water, wind."

DAN JENKINS

"All that matters in golf is the next shot."

RALPH GULDAHL

"I see no reason why a golf course cannot be played in 18 birdies. Just because no one has ever done that doesn't mean it can't be done."

BEN HOGAN

"Putting is like wisdom — partly a natural gift, and partly the accumulation of experience."

ARNOLD PALMER

"The only shots you can be dead sure of are those you've already taken."

BYRON NELSON

"I PLAY WITH FRIENDS,

BUT WE DON'T PLAY

FRIENDLY GAMES."

BEN HOGAN

"There is no such thing as natural touch.
Touch is something you create by hitting
millions of golf balls."

LEE TREVINO

"I never played a round when I didn't learn
something new about the game."

BEN HOGAN

"There are no guarantees in this game — not to
mention this life — and we have only a short
time to enjoy it. Even when I'm not playing
particularly well, I enjoy what I do."

SCOTT SIMPSON

"Play happy."

NANCY LOPEZ'S FATHER TO HER WHEN SHE WAS YOUNG

"Confidence is everything.
From there it's a small step to winning."

CRAIG STADLER

"If there is any larceny in a man,
golf will bring it out."

PAUL GALLICO

"How would you like to meet the top
143 people at what you do each week
in order to survive?"

BRUCE CRAMPTON

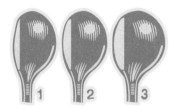

"The ideal build for a golfer would be strong hands, big forearms, thick neck, big thighs, and a flat chest. He'd look like Popeye."

GARY PLAYER

"This is a game of misses. The guy who misses best is going to win."

BEN HOGAN

"Some days I wonder about practice. I've hit about 70,000 golf balls in the last four years, and some days I still play like an amateur."

HUBERT GREEN

"Ninety percent of the putts that fall short
don't go in."

YOGI BERRA

"You drive for show and putt for dough."

BOBBY LOCKE

"The real way to enjoy playing golf
is to take pleasure not in the score,
but in the execution of the strokes."

BOBBY JONES

"Half of golf is fun; the other half is putting."

PETER DOBEREINER

"You need a fantastic memory in this game to remember the great shots, and a very short memory to forget the bad ones."

Mac O'Grady

"There's nothing natural about the golf swing."

Ben Hogan

"Practice puts brains in your muscles."

Sam Snead

"What other people may find in poetry,
I find in the flight of a good drive."

ARNOLD PALMER

"A lot of guys who have never choked
have never been in the position to do so."

TOM WATSON

"Golf is most assuredly a mystifying game.
It would seem that if a person has hit a golf ball
correctly a thousand times, he should be able
to duplicate the performance at will.
But such is certainly not the case."

BOBBY JONES

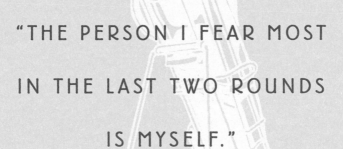

"THE PERSON I FEAR MOST

IN THE LAST TWO ROUNDS

IS MYSELF."

TOM WATSON

THE OBJECTS OF CONVERSATION

"When Jack Nicklaus plays well, he wins.
When he plays badly, he finishes second.
When he plays terribly, he finishes third."

JOHNNY MILLER

"Gray-blue, they had a piercing quality.
They were the eyes of a circling bird of prey:
fearless, fierce, the pupil no more than
a dot in their imperious center.
They were not the eyes of a loser."

SPORTSWRITER JIM MURRAY
ON THE EYES OF BEN HOGAN

"The three things I fear the most in golf are
lightning, Ben Hogan, and a downhill putt."

SAM SNEAD

"If that guy ever wins a tournament,
it will set golf back 100 years."

PGA CHAMP CHICK HARBERT,
WATCHING NEWCOMER ARNOLD PALMER
AT THE '54 U.S. AMATEUR

"The ball's scared of him.
He'll get it in the hole if he has to scare it in."

BOB ROSBURG ON THE PLAY OF ARNOLD PALMER

"Michael Jordan strikes me as one of the
greatest athletes who ever lived, but Sam
Snead still goes down as the greatest. He's
performed in his teens, his twenties, his
thirties, his forties, his fifties, his sixties,
and at seventy he finished second."

GARY PLAYER

ON THE MASTERS

"We wanted to make bogeys easy if frankly sought,
pars readily obtainable by standard good play, and
birdies, except on par fives, dearly bought."

BOBBY JONES

"The Masters is the only tournament I ever
knew where you choke when you drive
through the front gate."

GARY PLAYER

"There's no other golf course like this anywhere.
Never has been. Its greens and its challenges on and
around the greens are just super, super tough.
So they are fun to play, in sort of a morbid way."

BEN CRENSHAW

JUST FOR FUN

"Golf fairways should be made more narrow.
Then everyone would have to play from
the rough, not just me."

SEVE BALLESTEROS

"Give me a man with big hands, big feet, and no
brains, and I will make a golfer out of him."

WALTER HAGEN

"Mr. Agnew, I believe you have a slight
swing in your flaw."

JIMMY DEMARET TO PLAYING PARTNER
VICE PRESIDENT SPIRO AGNEW

"Prayer never seems to work for me on the
golf course. I think this has something to do
with my being a terrible putter."

THE REV. BILLY GRAHAM

"A driving range is the place where golfers go
to get all of the good shots out of their system."

HUMORIST HENRY BEARD

"I won't say my golf is bad, but if I started growing tomatoes, they'd come up sliced!"

MILLER BARBER

"The game was easy for me as a kid. I had to play awhile to find out how hard it is."

RAYMOND FLOYD

"I would like to think of myself as an athlete first, but I don't want to do a disservice to the real ones."

DAVID DUVAL

"The older I get, the better I used to be."

LEE TREVINO

"Columbus went around the world in 1492.
That isn't a lot of strokes when you
consider the course."

LEE TREVINO

"I play in the low 80s. If it's any hotter
than that, I won't play."

BOXING GREAT JOE LOUIS

"I was three over — one over a house, one over
a patio, and one over a swimming pool."

GEORGE BRETT ON HIS GOLF GAME

"If you think it's hard to meet new people,
try picking up the wrong golf ball."

JACK LEMMON

"If I'm on the course and lightning starts,
I get inside fast. If God wants to play through,
let him."

BOB HOPE

"THE ONLY REASON I
PLAYED GOLF WAS SO
I COULD AFFORD TO GO
HUNTING OR FISHING."

SAM SNEAD

"I never exaggerate, I just remember big."

CHI CHI RODRIGUEZ

"If it wasn't for golf, I don't know what
I'd be doing. If my IQ had been two points
lower, I'd have been a plant somewhere."

LEE TREVINO

"The safest place would be in the fairway."

JOE GARAGIOLA ON THE BEST PLACE
FOR SPECTATORS TO STAND
DURING CELEBRITY GOLF TOURNAMENTS

"The rest of the field."

ROGER MALTBIE WHEN ASKED WHAT HE NEEDED
TO SHOOT TO WIN A TOURNAMENT

"Still your shot."

DAVE MARR ON THE THREE UGLIEST WORDS IN GOLF

"His driving is unbelievable.
I don't go that far on my holidays."

IAN BAKER-FINCH ON JOHN DALY

"It took me 17 years to get 3,000 hits.
I did it in one afternoon on the golf course."

BASEBALL LEGEND HANK AARON

"I can airmail the golf ball, but sometimes I don't put the right address on it."

JIM DENT

"You can't call it a sport. You don't run, jump, you don't shoot, you don't pass. All you have to do is buy some clothes that don't match."

STEVE SAX

"It's nice to look down the fairway and see your mother on the left and your father on the right. You know that no matter whether you hook it or slice it, somebody is going to be there to kick it back in the fairway."

LARRY NELSON

"I'll take a two-shot penalty. But I'll be darned if
I'm going to play the ball where it lies."

ELAINE JOHNSON AFTER HER TEE SHOT HIT A TREE
AND CAROMED INTO HER BRA

"My swing is so bad, I look like a caveman
killing his lunch."

LEE TREVINO

"I needed 'em both."

BASKETBALL HALL OF FAMER BOB LANIER
ON PLAYING GOLF WITH A DOCTOR AND A PRIEST

"You're a good loser if you can grip the winner's
hand without wishing it was his throat."

SPORTSWRITER HAL CHADWICK

"Golf combines two favorite American pastimes:
taking long walks and hitting things with a stick."

P. J. O'ROURKE

"We have 51 golf courses in Palm Springs.
He never decides which one of them he will
play until after his first tee shot."

BOB HOPE ON GERALD FORD

"My best score is 103.
But I've only been playing 15 years."

ALEX KARRAS

"Like a lot of fellows around here, I have furniture
problems. My chest has fallen into my drawers."

BILLY CASPER ON THE SENIOR TOUR

"I'm hitting the woods just great, but I'm having a terrible time getting out of them."

HARRY TOSCANO

"Why am I using a new putter? Because the old one didn't float too well."

CRAIG STADLER

SCORECARD

FAST FACTS & RECORDS

With more than 17,300, the United States has more golf courses than any other country. (Worldwide, there are an estimated 30,000 courses.)

All of Europe has just under 6,000 courses, and China, home to over 1.2 billion people, has just 100 golf courses.

It is estimated that more than 50 million people worldwide play golf. Their average score for a round is 107.

Golf courses are among the top five public places in America for the occurrence of heart attacks.

South African Gary Player figures he has flown
more than 14 million air miles over his career
and estimates he has spent the equivalent of
$3\frac{1}{2}$ to 4 years sitting on an airplane.

Back in the 1990s, the stock exchange always
went up on the Monday after Tiger Woods
played in a tournament the day before.
The stock market consistently jumped about
1.2 percent each Monday after Woods played
televised golf. That amounts to some $45 billion
in wealth created with the help of Mr. Woods.

Robert Gamez holds the record for most years
between tour victories with 15 years 6 months.
He won the Nestle Invitational at Bay Hill Club
in Orlando in 1990 and the Valero Texas Open
in San Antonio in 2005.

PGA MONEY LEADERS AT 10-YEAR INTERVALS

1955 — Julius Boros, $63,121.55

1965 — Jack Nicklaus, $140,752.14

1975 — Jack Nicklaus, $298,149.17

1985 — Curtis Strange, $542,321.00

1995 — Greg Norman, $1,654,959.00

2005 — Tiger Woods, $10,628,024.00

LEFT-HANDED GOLFERS WHO HAVE WON MAJORS

Bob Charles
BRITISH OPEN 1963

Mike Weir
MASTERS 2003

Phil Mickelson
MASTERS 2004, PGA 2005, AND MASTERS 2006

(All three of the above are actually right-handed outside of golf.)

While Tiger Woods is the youngest golfer
(21 years 3 months) to win the Masters
(in 1997), check out the ages of the youngest
players to win the other three Majors:

1968 British Open

WON BY YOUNG TOM MORRIS AT 17 YEARS 5 MONTHS

1911 U.S. Open

WON BY JOHN J. McDERMOTT AT 19 YEARS 10
MONTHS

1922 PGA

WON BY GENE SARAZEN AT 20 YEARS 5 MONTHS

Sam Snead is the oldest winner in PGA history, winning the Greater Greensboro at 52 years 10 months in 1965.

Jack Nicklaus won the Masters at 46 years 2 months in 1986. Here are the five oldest PGA winners in the 1990s:

Ray Floyd
49 YEARS 6 MONTHS — 1992 DORAL

Hale Irwin
48 YEARS 9 MONTHS — 1994 MCI

Tom Watson
48 YEARS 8 MONTHS — 1998 COLONIAL

Ed Dougherty
47 YEARS 7 MONTHS — 1995 DEPOSIT

Tom Watson
46 YEARS 9 MONTHS — 1996 MEMORIAL

CAREER AWARDS PRESENTED TO JACK NICKLAUS
(NON-COMPREHENSIVE, BY THE WAY)

Gold Tee Award
METROPOLITAN GOLF ASSOCIATION OF NEW YORK, 1968

Honorary Doctorate
OHIO STATE UNIVERSITY, 1972

Inductee
WORLD GOLF HALL OF FAME, 1974

Bob Jones Award
USGA, 1975

Athlete of the Decade: 1970s
NATIONAL SPORTS WRITERS

Golfer of the 1970s
GOLF MAGAZINE

Sportsman of the Year
SPORTS ILLUSTRATED, 1978

BBC Overseas Sports Personality of the Year
1980

Honorary Doctorate
ST. ANDREWS UNIVERSITY, 1984

Providencia Award
PALM BEACH COUNTY, 1992
TO AN INDIVIDUAL WHO, OR ORGANIZATION WHICH, HAS MADE
A SIGNIFICANT CONTRIBUTION TO THE TOURISM INDUSTRY

Inductee
CANADIAN GOLF HALL OF FAME, 1995

Payne Stewart Award
PGA TOUR, 2000

Memorial Tournament Honoree
CAPTAINS CLUB, 2000

Distinguished Service Award
PGA OF AMERICA, 2000

Donald Ross Award
AMERICAN SOCIETY OF GOLF ARCHITECTS, 2001

Vince Lombardi Award of Excellence
2001

ESPY Lifetime Achievement Award
ESPN, 2001

Don A. Rossi Award
GOLF COURSE BUILDERS ASSOCIATION OF AMERICA, 2001

Florida Athlete of the Century
FLORIDA SPORTS AWARDS

Best Individual Male Athlete
of the Twentieth Century
SPORTS ILLUSTRATED

Golfer of the Century
GOLF MAGAZINE, GOLF DIGEST, GOLF WORLD, BBC

Muhammad Ali Sports Legend Award
2003

International Association of Golf Tourism Award
2004

continued on next page

Orthopedic Hospital
Paul Runyan Recognition Award
LOS ANGELES, 2005

Listener of the Year
INTERNATIONAL LISTENING ASSOCIATION, 2005

Old Tom Morris Award
GOLF COURSE SUPERINTENDENTS ASSOCIATION OF AMERICA, 2005

Japan's Foreign Minister's Commendation
IN COMMEMORATION OF THE 150TH ANNIVERSARY
OF THE U.S./JAPAN RELATIONSHIP, 2005

Royal Bank of Scotland Five Pound Note
2005

Michael Williams Award
ASSOCIATION OF GOLF WRITERS, 2005
FOR COOPERATION WITH AND SUPPORT OF BRITISH GOLF WRITERS

Distinguished Service Award
PGA OF AMERICA, 2000

Presidential Medal of Freedom
2005
THE HIGHEST CIVILIAN AWARD IN THE UNITED STATES

ASAP Sports/Jim Murray Award
GOLF WRITERS ASSOCIATION OF AMERICA, 2006
FOR COOPERATION WITH THE MEDIA

OTHER PRIZES AWARDED AT THE MASTERS

(BESIDES THE GREEN JACKET)

Gold Medal
WINNER

Silver Medal and Silver Salver
RUNNER-UP

Silver Cup
LOVE AMATEUR

Silver Medal
AMATEUR RUNNER-UP

Crystal Vase
EACH DAY'S LOW SCORE

Large Crystal Bowl
HOLE IN ONE

Pair of Crystal Goblets
EAGLE

Large Crystal Bowl
DOUBLE EAGLE

GOLF MAGAZINE'S 18 GREATEST GOLF HOLES IN THE WORLD

• PAR 3s •

Banff Springs Golf Course
BANFF, ALBERTA, CANADA — 4TH HOLE, 192 YARDS

Cypress Point Club
PEBBLE BEACH, CA — 15TH HOLE, 139 YARDS

National Golf Links of America
SOUTHAMPTON, NY — 4TH HOLE, 197 YARDS

TPC at Sawgrass
PONTE VEDRA BEACH, FL — 17TH HOLE, 132 YARDS

• PAR 4s •

Ballybunion Golf Club
BALLYBUNION, COUNTY KERRY, IRELAND —
11TH HOLE, 453 YARDS

Bethpage State Park (Black Course)
FARMINGDALE, NY — 5TH HOLE, 451 YARDS

Merion Golf Club (East)
ARDMORE, PA — 16TH HOLE, 428 YARDS

Mid Ocean Club
TUCKER'S TOWN, BERMUDA — 5TH HOLE, 433 YARDS

Pine Valley Golf Club
CLEMENTON, NJ — 13TH HOLE, 448 YARDS

Royal County Down Golf Club
NEWCASTLE, COUNTY DOWN, N. IRELAND —
9TH HOLE, 486 YARDS

Royal Melbourne Golf Club (West)
BLACK ROCK, MELBOURNE, AUSTRALIA —
6TH HOLE, 450 YARDS

continued on next page

St. Andrews (Old)
ST. ANDREWS, FIFE, SCOTLAND — 17TH HOLE, 461 YARDS

Shinnecock Hills Golf Club
SOUTHAMPTON, NY — 14TH HOLE, 447 YARDS

Southern Hills Country Club
TULSA, OK — 12TH HOLE, 445 YARDS

• PAR 5s •

Augusta National Golf Club
AUGUSTA, GA — 13TH HOLE, 510 YARDS

Carnoustie Golf Links
CARNOUSTIE, ANGUS, SCOTLAND — 6TH HOLE, 578 YARDS

Durban Country Club
DURBAN, NATAL, SOUTH AFRICA — 3RD HOLE, 513 YARDS

Pebble Beach Golf Links
PEBBLE BEACH, CA — 18TH HOLE, 548 YARDS

CELEBRITIES WHO HAVE
SCORED A HOLE IN ONE

Clint Eastwood

Supreme Court Justice Sandra Day O'Connor

Don Zimmer
(SHOT 135 FOR THE ROUND)

Kim Jon Il
A NORTH KOREAN MINISTER OF INFORMATION SAID IL'S
FIRST-ROUND TOTAL WAS 11 HOLES IN ONE

Charles Schwab

Carlton Fisk

Joe DiMaggio
ON A DAY HE ANNOUNCED HE'D DONATE A COLOR TV
TO WHOEVER MADE AN ACE

John Elway
ON HIS 40TH BIRTHDAY

Roger Clemens

Three U.S. Presidents:
Eisenhower, Nixon, and Ford

NAMES OF ST. ANDREWS
OLD COURSE HOLES

Burn

Dyke

Cartgate (out)

Ginger Beer

Hole O'Cross (out)

Heathery (out)

High (out)

Short

End

Bobby Jones

High (in)

Heathery (in)

Hole O'Cross (in)

Long

Cartgate (in)

Corner of the Dyke

Road

Tom Morris

NAMES OF
AUGUSTA NATIONAL HOLES

Tea Olive

Pink Dogwood

Flowering Peach

Flowering Crab Apple

Magnolia

Juniper

Pampas

Yellow Jasmine

Carolina Cherry

Camellia

White Dogwood

Golden Bell

Azalea

Chinese Fir

Firethorn

Redbud

Nandina

Holly

FAVORITE GOLF NICKNAMES

The Golden Bear
JACK NICKLAUS

Lord Byron
BYRON NELSON

Lefty
PHIL MICKELSON

Tiger
ELDRICK WOODS

The Shark
GREG NORMAN

Fuzzy
FRANK ZOELLER

The Squire
GENE SARAZEN

Boom Boom
FRED COUPLES

The Walrus
CRAIG STADLER

Lumpy
TIM HERRON

El Niño
SERGIO GARCIA

Slammin' Sammy
SAM SNEAD

Chi Chi
JUAN RODRIGUEZ

The Wild Thing
JOHN DALY

The Big Easy
ERNIE ELS

Radar
MIKE REID

The Merry Mex
LEE TREVINO

MOST APPROPRIATE
GOLFER NICKNAMES

Tommy Armour: Silver Scot
BORN IN EDINBURGH, HE HAD SILVER-WHITE HAIR

Miller Barber: X
INSCRUTABLE BEHIND HIS SUNGLASSES

Tommy Bolt: Terrible Tommy or Thunder Bolt
KNOWN FOR HIS TEMPER

Gay Brewer: Hound Dog
HE LOOKED LIKE ONE

Bob Charles: Sphinx of the Links
SAID VERY LITTLE

Ben Crenshaw: Gentle Ben
MILD-MANNERED AND COURTLY

John Daly: The Wild Thing
NO EXPLANATION REQUIRED

Al Geiberger: Skippy
ATE PEANUT BUTTER SANDWICHES ON THE COURSE

Bobby Jones: The Emperor
NO EXPLANATION NEEDED

Tony Lema: Champagne Tony
ORDERED CHAMPAGNE FOR WRITERS AFTER WINNING
1964 BRITISH OPEN

Gene Littler: Gene the Machine
FOR HIS METRONOMIC SWING

Johnny Miller: Desert Fox
FOR HIS DOMINATION OF DESERT COURSES WHILE WINNING
IN ARIZONA IN THE EARLY 1970S

Colin Montgomerie: Mrs. Doubtfire
CURLY, HIGH HAIRSTYLE AND GENERAL LUMPINESS INVITED THIS
NICKNAME AFTER THE CHARACTER PLAYED BY ROBIN WILLIAMS
IN THE MOVIE OF THE SAME NAME

Tom Shaw: Technicolor Tommy
FOR HIS COLORFUL WARDROBE

GOLFER SUPERSTITIONS

Charles Howell III always tees up the ball
in such a way that the clubhead will smack
the ball's brand name.

Justin Leonard will always mark with
the same coin — until he misses an easy putt.

Michael Clark II tries to wear underwear
with holes in them.

Mike Weir says he puts his putter in the toilet
overnight to wash away the "evil lip-out curse."

Jesper Parnevik will never mark his ball with
a coin faced heads-up.

Payne Stewart never used a ball again
after making a bogey with it.

Ernie Els is through with a ball after hitting
one birdie with it.

Tom Weiskopf uses broken tees on par threes.

Jack Nicklaus always carries three coins in his pocket.

HANDICAPPING WEBSTER: A GOLFER'S DICTIONARY

ACE: A hole made in one stroke.

ADDRESS: Position of a player who has taken a stance over the ball and grounded the club preparatory to striking the ball.

APRON: The grassy area bordering the green, with grass longer than the green but shorter than the fairway; also known as the fringe.

BACKSPIN: Backward rotation of a ball caused by striking it with a downward blow.

BANANA BALL: A slice that curves to the right in the shape of a banana. An extreme slice.

BEACH: Sand hazard on a course.

BIRD'S NEST: A lie in which the ball is cupped in deep grass.

BUZZARD: A score of two strokes over par on a hole.

continued on next page

CADDIE: Someone who carries a player's golf bag, locates the driven ball and, on occasion, offers advice.

CARPET: The putting green, or the fairway.

CARRY: Distance a ball travels in the air.

CHILI-DIP: To hit the ground before the ball, producing a weak lofted shot.

COLLAR: The grassy fringe surrounding the putting green.

CONDOR: A four-under-par shot. A hole in one on a par 5, for example. Has occurred on a hole with a heavy dogleg, hard ground, and no trees. Might also be called "a triple eagle."

DANCE FLOOR: For the green. As in "you're on the dance floor."

DAWN PATROL: Golfers who tee off early to avoid the heavy traffic.

DOGLEG: A left or right bend in the fairway.

DRAW SHOT: Shot that travels straight, slightly to the right of the target, then curves inward to the left; a controlled hook.

DUFFER: An unskilled golfer. Also called a hacker.

EAGLE: Two strokes under par for a single hole. To play a hole at two under par.

FADE: Left to right direction of a shot, opposite to the draw shot; a modified slice.

FAN: To miss the ball completely.

FLASH TRAP: A shallow and small sand bunker.

FLIER: A ball is hit without spin and goes for a greater distance than normal.

FORE: A warning shouted out to warn anyone who may be in danger from the flight of the ball.

FRIED-EGG: A ball half-buried in the sand.

continued on next page

GIMME: A putt that is certain to be made on the next shot and will most likely be conceded by an opponent.

HACK: To chop violently at the ball; to make bad shots; to play bad golf.

HANDICAP: The number of strokes a player may deduct from his actual score to adjust his scoring ability to the level of a scratch golfer. It is designed to allow golfers of different abilities to basically compete on the same level.

HOG'S BACK: A ridge of ground or a hole having a ridge on a fairway.

HOLE IN ONE: Striking the ball from the tee into the hole in one stroke.

JUNGLE: A slang term for heavy rough.

KICK: Another term for "bounce" — usually an unpredictable or erratic bounce.

LINKS: Originally meaning a seaside course, it is now used to mean any golf course.

LOOSE IMPEDIMENTS: Any natural object that is not fixed or growing. This can include loose stones, twigs, branches, molehills, dung, worms, and insects.

MULLIGAN: Free shot sometimes allowed after a poor drive.

OVERCLUB: To use a club that gives too much distance.

PILL: Nickname for the ball.

PIN: Same as "flagstick."

POP-UP: A short, high shot.

QUAIL HIGH: A shot hit on a low and flat trajectory.

RIFLE: To play a shot accurately and for a great distance.

RUN: The distance the ball rolls on the ground.

SANDY: Making par after being in a bunker.

SCRATCH PLAYER: A player who has no handicap.

SHANK: Shot in which the ball is hit by the heel of the clubface and flies off-line to the right.

SKULLING: Hitting the ball at or above its center, causing the ball to be hit too hard and travel too great a distance.

continued on next page

SKY: To hit underneath the ball, sending it much higher than intended. Like a pop fly in baseball.

SLICE: A shot that curves strongly from left to right as a result of sidespin. The converse applies to a left-handed player.

SMOTHER: To hit down on the ball so that it travels a short distance on the ground.

SNAKE: A very long putt that travels over several breaks in the green.

SPOON: A 3-wood.

TEXAS WEDGE: What the putter is called when it's used from off the green. Also a shot played with a putter from outside the putting green.

TIGER TEE: A slang expression for the back tee.

WAGGLE: Movement of the clubhead prior to swinging — a flourishing of the club behind and over the ball.

WHIFF: To swing and miss the ball completely.

WINDCHEATER: A shot played low against the wind. It is played with strong backspin and starts low and rises only toward the end of the shot.

WINTER RULES: Practice of improving the lie of a ball by moving it to a better position because of poor turf condition. Not endorsed by the USGA.

WORMBURNER: A ball hit with adequate distance that hugs the ground.

YIP: To mis-hit a putt due to an attack of nerves, or "yips."

YIPS: Shakiness or nervousness in making a shot.

ZOOMIE: A drive that goes farther than most drives ever hit by the golfer who smacked it.

TIGER TALES

Tiger Woods is the greatest golfer of the
twenty-first century. But for all his fame,
you may not know everything about him.
For example...

After winning his second Masters in 2001,
club officials decided to redesign the course
in an attempt to "Tiger proof" Augusta.
Tiger returned the next year to win
back-to-back green jackets — then won
a fourth in 2005.

In 1996, he was named PGA Rookie of the Year
and *SI*'s Sportsman of the Year.

Tiger's actual scoring average of 68.17 in 2000
(the "Tiger Slam" year) was the lowest in
PGA Tour history, besting Byron Nelson's
68.33 average in 1945.

In 2005, Tiger earned an estimated $87 million.

continued on next page

On June 15, 1997, Tiger was named the top golfer in the world by the Official World Golf Rankings for the first time. He did this in just his forty-second week as a professional, the fastest ascent ever to the top spot.

He is the only golfer to be named PGA Player of the Year in the year following his rookie season.

At age 30 years 7 months, Woods became the youngest player to amass 50 PGA Tour wins.

In all of his major tournament victories,
Woods has held the outright lead or a share
of the lead after the third round.

A Tiger Woods rookie trading card from 1996
sold for $125,000 in 2001. Today, according to
card graders, the card is worth around $400.

MULLIGANS

HUMOROUS QUOTES
& ANECDOTES

Once, during the Bob Hope Classic at the Indian Wells Country Club, Gary Hallberg hit a shot that bounced off the cart path and bounded up on the roof of the clubhouse. By rule, Hallberg was permitted a free drop from the roof. Yet he realized that the only clear shot he had at the green was from up on the roof. So he pulled his wedge out of his bag and dropped a perfectly struck shot on the green. From there, he sunk a par putt.

In 1921, Peter McGregor won a match on the final hole at Scarborough South Cliff Course in Yorkshire, England — with an assist from an insect. McGregor and his opponent, Henry Dowie, were even as they played the final hole. McGregor needed to sink a long putt to win. His putt was on-line, but stopped right on the edge of the cup. Just then, a grasshopper jumped onto the ball and knocked it into the cup.

At the 1988 U.S. Women's Open, play was moving so slowly that golfer Lori Garbacz decided she would do something outlandish to make a point. At the 14th hole of the first round, she had her caddie go to a nearby pay phone and order a pizza to be delivered to her at the 17th tee. When Garbacz reached 17, the pizza was there waiting for her. Adding to her frustration, Garbacz had ample time to eat the pizza, as there were two groups ahead of her waiting to tee off.

A popular practice round betting game on Tour is called "thousand dollar no bogeys." The pros each commit to paying anyone in their respective foursome $1,000 if they make it through the practice round without a single bogey. It's particularly tough at major venues like Scotland's Turnberry, where in 1994, Corey Pavin, Ben Crenshaw, Davis Love III, and Brad Faxon agreed to a game. Crenshaw was out on the second hole, Love on the 12th, and Pavin a couple of holes later. That left Faxon against three guys with a vested interest in seeing him blow up. Faxon, in an interview with *Golf Digest*, said that what ensued was one of the greatest times he's ever had on a golf course: "During those last four holes, the three of them were rooting against me out loud right to the point of contact. As soon as I hit my ball on 18, I offered them each a buyout for $975. Nobody took it. I made my par and they all paid me $1,000. It took a while, but I got a check from every one of them."

Veteran golf writer T. R. Reinman recalls
meeting Phil Mickelson when the kid was
just 14. Reinman bet Mickelson a Coke that
he (Reinman) could hit a driving range fence
250 yards out, which he did. Then Mickelson
bet him two Cokes that he (Mickelson) could
do it with any club in Reinman's bag, even
though the writer is right-handed and Mickelson
is a lefty. Mickelson pulled out Reinman's driver,
turned it so the toe of the club faced down,
and smacked the ball 250 yards left-handed.
The lesson? Don't bet with Mickelson when
he's thirsty.

A New Zealand Web site that carried details
on the time and date of every round played by
all registered golfers in the country was closed
down in 2001, when players complained that
their bosses were finding out that they'd been
out golfing when they were supposed to be in
the office or at business meetings.

Arnold Palmer has given plenty of lessons,
but none was as costly as the one he gave
Davis Love III at Palmer's 1999 Bay Hill
Invitational. Love, who admits to having less
than lovely on-course temper tantrums, hit an
errant bunker shot. His next shot, however, was
right on target. He clobbered a sprinkler head
with his club and sent a gusher of water into the
sky. He said he deserved to be fined, and Palmer
obliged with a repair bill for $175,003.50 —
$3.50 for parts and $175,000 for labor.

As a publicity stunt before the 1977 Lancôme
Trophy Tournament in Paris, Arnold Palmer
hit three balls from the second stage of the
Eiffel Tower, more than 300 feet above the
ground. As the locals looked on, Palmer smacked
a drive 403 yards, then sent another one even
farther — when it hooked into an open-air
double-decker bus and took a ride for an
extra block.

The well-known expression to "whiff" the ball originated in 1876, when Lord Gormley Whiffle completely missed a four-inch putt to lose the Silver Medal at St. Andrews's Old Course. Spectators at the tournament kept remarking to one another, "Did you see that Whiffle?" Later the phrase was shortened to its present form.

The first time Frank Sinatra played a round of golf with Arnold Palmer, the crooner spent more time in the Palm Springs roughs than on the well-manicured fairways. After his tumultuous round, Sinatra had the nerve to ask Palmer, "What do you think of my game?" Palmer didn't hesitate as he turned to Sinatra and said "Not bad...but I still prefer golf."

The Wilson Sporting Goods Company sent
Masters champion Gene Sarazen to the 1954
U.S. Amateur championship at the Country
Club in Detroit to observe and critique a
young golfer. "He lunged at the ball, and he
duck-hooked everything," Sarazen recalled.
"He had to hole long putts and get up and
down out of the sand to win the title. I told
Wilson the kid would never amount to much."
That kid was Arnold Palmer.

Gary Player was practicing a difficult shot out
of a bunker at the ninth hole at Oakland Hills
while getting ready for the 1961 U.S. Open.
He was exploding shot after shot to within a
few feet of his target on the green. A spectator
who had been watching said, "Gee, are you ever
lucky!" Player responded, "Yes, and the more
I practice, the luckier I get."

Champions Tour veteran Sammy Rachels called his 3-iron his "mother-in-law club." When asked why he gave the club that moniker, he replied, "It's my mother-in-law club because I want to hit it, but I can't."

Along with his wife and children, Jesper Parnevik has been known to include in his gallery following some attractive young nannies who have the task of helping with Parnevik's children while he plays. Among those nannies was Elin Nordegren, a part-time model from Sweden. No sooner did Nordegren show up in the gallery than one Tiger Woods began to inquire about her. In 2002, Woods and Nordegren began dating and, shortly thereafter, were married. It was Parnevik who had introduced the two. "The original plan was to get Tiger distracted," says Parnevik. "But it hasn't seemed to work."

The longest period between PGA victories by one golfer belongs to Butch Baird. After winning the 1961 Waco Turner Open, it took Baird 15 years 5 months and 10 days before he won again at the 1976 San Antonio Texas Open. Ed Fiori nearly matched Baird's record for perseverance. His victory at the 1996 Quad City Classic was his first on Tour since the 1982 Bob Hope Desert Classic — a span of 14 years 8 months and 2 days.

In 1998, during the second round at the Players Championship, a seagull picked Brad Fabel's ball off the island green and dropped it into the nearby water hazard. By rule, Fabel was allowed to place a new ball where the old one had first come to rest. But he still bogeyed the hole.

Between 1923 and 1930, the year he retired from tournament golf at age 28, Bobby Jones finished first or second in the U.S. Open every year except 1927. He also won three British Opens, a British Amateur, and five U.S. Amateurs. In the quarter-finals, semifinals, and finals of those five U.S. Amateurs, Jones stood a total of 136 holes up on his 15 opponents — meaning he won those 15 36-hole matches by an average of 9 and 8.

Jerry Barber put on one of the most remarkable putting displays in a major tournament during the 1961 PGA Championship. As darkness began to fall, Barber trailed Don January by four strokes with only three holes to play. He then sank successive putts of 22 feet, 44 feet, and 58 feet — two for birdies and one for par — to tie the stunned January. Barber then beat January the following day in the playoff.

In the first round of the 1927 British Open, Bobby Jones needed only 28 putts. He did not miss a putt under 12 feet and drained 6 from more than 100 feet. On the 5th hole, Jones sank a putt that was paced off at 120 feet.

Mac O'Grady began trying for his Tour card in 1971 and failed at Qualifying School a record 16 times before finally making it in 1982 on his 17th try. His story is a study in perseverance. During his annual attempt to become a Tour pro, O'Grady supported himself by working as a cook, dishwasher, busboy, caddie, and funeral home worker. Persistence paid off for O'Grady, as by 1990, he had won over $1 million on the Tour.

Ben Hogan never forgot the turning point of his golf career — and his life. It occurred in 1938, when he and his wife were down to their last $85. "If I didn't win money at the Oakland Open, I was through," Hogan recalled. "The night before the tournament started, someone stole the two rear wheels off my car. I had to hitch a ride to play. But I shot a 69 in the last round and tied for third. The $385 I won enabled me to put wheels back on my car and keep going." From that point on, Hogan began his rise to become one of the greatest golfers of all time.

When Walter Hagen was about to play in the 1925 PGA Championship at Olympia Fields outside Chicago, he walked into the locker room before the tournament and confronted opponents Leo Diegel and Al Watrous. In a loud voice, the ultraconfident Hagen asked, "Well, who's going to be second?" He then went out and beat the two golfers in match play and won the championship.

In 1876, David Strath bet all comers he could negotiate the bunkers and huge greens of the Old Course at St. Andrews in fewer than 100 strokes — while playing in the dark. With only a full moon and those who took him up on the wager accompanying him, Strath shot 95 and didn't lose a single ball. In his memory, the front bunker on the 11th hole at St. Andrews was named the Strath Bunker.

In 2002, professional golf witnessed what was perhaps the greatest single season any pro golfer — male or female — has ever had. And it came in the play of Annika Sorenstam. In virtually every category, Sorenstam was a better golfer than Tiger Woods. She won an astounding 48 percent of the tournaments she entered. She won more than 10 percent of all the purses for the year, and her average margin of victory was 3.27 strokes. Sorenstam won 13 overall titles in 2002, equaling the record set by Mickey Wright in 1963. She averaged 68.7 strokes per round, breaking her own record of 69.42, and she earned $2.86 million — another record.

MOON SHOTS

February 15, 1971, stands as a momentous day in history. Not only was it the day man first walked on the moon, it was also the day that saw the longest golf shot in history. The two events occurred in the same place.

Astronaut Alan Shepard was a golf fanatic. The first American launched into outer space, Shepard was commander of the Lunar Landing Mission in 1971. Upon boarding the spacecraft, Shepard managed to sneak in a cut-down 6-iron

continued on next page

and two golf balls. When the lunar module landed on the moon six days after the Apollo 14 crew launched into space, Shepard became the fifth American to walk on the moon. He decided to play a little golf while he was there.

Shepard had managed to rig a club from four pieces of aluminum and his piece of 6-iron. He had two obstacles — his spacesuit was so big and bulky that he had to swing his "club" with just one arm. The lie wasn't very good either, with the moon's surface being like a giant sand trap.

He scuffed his first shot, yet because of the moon's atmosphere, it traveled about 200 yards. He shanked his second shot and then threw his club. Still Shepard recalls the experience fondly: "The ball went miles and miles and miles."

Comedian Bob Hope recalled something else from Shepard's walk back to the module. "Something lying in the dust caught his eye," Hope said. "It was another golf ball — with Jerry Ford's name on it."

The 1965 U.S. Open at Bellerive provided the
setting for the first color telecast of a U.S. Open
golf tournament. In order to make the course
look better for the television audience viewing
at home, tournament officials spray-painted the
last two greens. Their choice of paint color?
Green.

Tour pro Frank Nobilo was playing a round
at Lake Nona Golf and Country Club near
Orlando, FL, when he was hit above the left
eye by an errant shot. The gash needed 30
stitches to close. The injury resulted in Nobilo's
needing to wear an eye patch for a brief time —
a fitting look for a man who is the descendant
of Italian pirates.

DON'T DESPISE
HUMBLE BEGINNINGS

Some of golf's top players began playing the game in circumstances less than ideal for future pros.

Four-time British Open champion Willie Park Jr. learned to putt on the brick floor of his Scottish home. After mastering the way of brick and mortar, he said most greens were easy.

During Chi Chi Rodriguez's childhood in Puerto Rico, he used a tree branch for a club and a smashed tin can for a ball. He would hit the can around the streets for hours with his friends. This practice served to form a basis for his incredible shot-making expertise.

Jim Dent grew up in a poor neighborhood near the Augusta National course. He and his friends would watch play through the fence and then create a makeshift course in the dirt lots, digging holes in the ground to aim for.

Jonathan Byrd's errant tee shot in the final round of the 2002 Buick Challenge hit his fiancée, Amanda Talley, on the left shoulder. This turned out to be a good thing for Byrd, as the ball ricocheted off Talley's shoulder, onto the cart path, coming to rest in a favorable lie in the rough just off the 5th hole. With his fiancée okay, Byrd went on to win the tournament by one stroke. A month later, Byrd and Talley were married.

Bobby Locke, regarded as the greatest putter in golf history, went the entire 1948 season without three-putting a single green in tournament competition.

Jack Nicklaus is considered by most as the
twentieth century's greatest player. And anyone
who watched a young Nicklaus play wouldn't
be surprised. He shot 51 for his first 9 holes, at
age 10. At 11, he shot 81 for 18 holes. By age
12, he routinely broke 80. At 13, he was a
three-handicapper and had broken 70. By age
16, he had won the Ohio Amateur. And at 19,
he won the first of his two U.S. Amateur titles.

Tiger Woods owes a debt of gratitude to a
waitress for helping him win the 2000 Canadian
Open. He almost was disqualified for missing
the start of the round because he and his caddie
thought the tee time was 8:57 a.m. instead of
7:57 a.m. Woods was in a restaurant waiting for
an omelet, unaware that his playing partners were
on the practice range getting ready. Luckily, the
waitress was thinking for Woods, he explained
afterward. "The lady came up to me and says,
'Well, you have fifteen minutes until your tee
time.'" He raced out to the course and made
it to the first tee with only a minute to spare.

Mark Calcavecchia is known to have a sour demeanor on the course, yet he insists he is not an unhappy guy. "I'm the happiest guy in the world 19 hours a day," he says. "It's the five hours I'm out on the golf course that I'm miserable. But that's not bad when you're happy most of the day."

You wouldn't blame the Jubelirer family of Sharon, PA, if they put up a shrine at the par 3 9th hole at Squaw Creek Country Club in Vienna, OH. Incredibly, all four members of the family have aced that particular hole. Mark Jubelirer aced the hole first in 1970. Then mom Natalie got hers in 1993. It was dad Harry's turn in 1997, and finally, Mark's brother Steven found the cup in 2001.

During an exhibition golf match between baseball superstars Babe Ruth and Ty Cobb, Cobb beat Ruth, 3 and 2. Ever the competitor, Cobb practiced for weeks before facing Ruth. The win meant so much to him that he placed the rather cheap victory trophy right next to his Hall of Fame plaque on his mantel at home. Ruth took the defeat in stride. In fact, his goal for the match was simply to have fun — and entertain the gallery all along the way.

During the 1939 U.S. Open, Byron Nelson hit the pin six times with shots from either the tee or fairway. Not one of those shots dropped in the cup for a hole in one or an eagle. Each of the shots was struck with a different club: a wedge, 9-iron, 6-iron, 4-iron, 1-iron, and driver. Nelson finished the final round tied for the lead, which led to an 18-hole playoff. Nelson won that playoff, shooting a 70 that included an eagle on the par-4 4th hole — another shot that clipped the pin. Nelson said that had he lost, it would have been one of the most frustrating defeats of his career.

Perhaps the greatest pro golfer no one has ever
heard of, Billy Dunk was a phenomenal player
internationally during the 1960s and 1970s.
The Aussie won more than 100 tournaments
during that span, including five Australian PGA
championships, and broke 80 course records.
Speculation ran rampant as to how Dunk would
do playing in America against the likes of
Palmer and Nicklaus. Yet Dunk never traveled
to America because he did not like flying.
So the debate continues as to just how good
Dunk really was.

Ray Floyd, on turning 50 and becoming eligible for the PGA Senior Tour, said, "I went to bed on September 4, 1992, and I was old and washed up. I woke up a rookie. What could be better?" After becoming eligible for the Senior Tour, Floyd won his first senior tournament the following Sunday. That made him the first golfer in history to win on both the PGA and Senior Tour in the same year — as he had won the PGA Tour's Doral Ryder Open in March of 1992.

Arnold Palmer used a 5-iron to ace the 182 yard 3rd hole at the TPC at Avenel during the 1989 Chrysler Cup Pro-Am in Potomac, MD. The next day a TV crew showed up at the hole and told Arnie they were there to film a piece about his hole in one. "You're a day late," Arnie said. "That was yesterday." Arnie, ever the accommodating one, agreed to try to re-create the shot. So he drew out his 5-iron and, while the camera rolled, he aced it again. Recalled Palmer, "You should have seen the crowd around the hole on the third day."

Long-driving champion Viktor Johansson
routinely hits a golf ball more than 420 yards.
His clubhead speed has been clocked at 165 miles
per hour. Most top pros measure out at about
110 mph — and Johansson breaks driver shafts
or caves in clubheads at least once a week.
At long driving shows he's billed as "Swing
Kong." The 6-foot-6, 275-pound golfer from
Delray Beach, FL, wows crowds by hitting
a ball through a phone book and a $3/4$-inch
piece of plywood. The amazing thing is, the ball
compresses so much to get through the plywood
that it makes a hole actually smaller than the ball
itself. A ball can't be passed through the hole.
This passion for power began in 1988 when, at
age 11, Viktor began playing at a local club in his
native country of Sweden. Equally spectacular was
his first round of golf, which included an eagle
on the course's opening hole.

GOING
FOR THE
GREEN

AMAZING EFFORTS
& VICTORIES

THE MASTER

In a game that has become dominated by twenty-somethings, golfers in their late thirties are often considered past their prime. Forty is old, and by golf standards, 46 is ancient. So it's no wonder that Jack Nicklaus had plenty of skeptics as he began the 1986 Masters.

Nicklaus entered the tournament on the heels of a long slump. He had missed the cut in three of seven tournaments that year and had withdrawn from a fourth. He hadn't won a tournament in two years, a Major in six. So it appeared that he was simply another long-shot golfer arriving at Augusta that week.

Some golf pundits chose to announce this as fact. Columnist Tom McCollister of the *Atlanta Journal-Constitution* had this to say: "Nicklaus is gone, done. He just doesn't have the game anymore. It's rusted from lack of use. He's 46, and nobody that old wins the Masters."

Twenty-three years prior to this tournament, Nicklaus had won his first green jacket at age 23. He now set out to win his sixth by proving that experience could beat youth. Three days into the event, youth was winning. After 54 holes, Nicklaus was down by four strokes, and the eight golfers in front of him had combined for 21 major championships. But as Nicklaus knew, golf legends are made on Sundays, never before.

As he followed his tee shot of his final round into the fairway on that fateful April day, Nicklaus walked with a spring in his step that no one had seen in years. He was the Golden Bear reborn.

"When I got it going, I believed I could make it happen," Nicklaus remembered.

Birdie followed birdie, and Nicklaus marched back into contention. By the ninth hole, his gallery had grown to twice its original size. Fans whispered back and forth, wondering if this could really be happening.

continued on next page

An eagle on 15 increased his momentum. The next hole, however, would prove to be the shot of the tournament. On the difficult par 3, he struck the ball hard with a 5-iron. His son Jackie, who was also acting as his caddie, begged the 5-iron to "be the right club." Nicklaus, in his finest moment, gave his son a knowing wink and a confident "It is." He put the ball three feet from the pin.

"There was electricity in the air that I've still not ever seen [since]," said Jim Nantz of CBS Sports.

About this time, 29-year-old Seve Ballesteros was in the lead at seven under par, one hole behind Nicklaus. After hearing the roaring ovation when Nicklaus holed out ahead of him, Ballesteros put his second shot in the drink and opened the door for the Golden Bear. Nicklaus then hit a 12-foot putt for birdie on 17, earning him his first lead of the tournament. The gallery erupted.

"The roar from 17 when Jack's putt fell remains the loudest sound I've ever heard on a golf course," Nick Price told *Golf Digest*. "The noise, the people running in all directions, the energy in the air...I've never experienced anything like it."

In the end, experience, and perhaps fate, won the day. Nicklaus finished with a remarkable 65 in the final round, made possible by a divine 30 on the back nine. His lead proved to be enough,

continued on next page

as he won his sixth Masters by one stroke over Tom Kite and Greg Norman. At age 46, he was the oldest Masters champion in the tournament's storied history.

What's more, Nicklaus earned the right for a friendly "I told you so." Who was the first person that Nicklaus asked for after his victory? A certain sports writer from Atlanta — Tom McCollister.

It has often been called the greatest Masters of all time. It is no doubt one of Nicklaus's personal favorites.

"You had the excitement of the golf tournament," he recalled. "You have to control your emotions; you have to be aggressive — it's not always that easy to pull all those together. But when you do, it's a blast."

THE EYE OF THE TIGER

Over the 2001-2002 golf seasons, Tiger Woods won all four professional majors in succession — marking the only time that a player has held all four major championship titles at the same time. There was a time when golf went 19 straight majors without ever having a repeat winner, much less a four-times-in-a-row winner. Thus, the "Tiger Slam" stands as one of golf's most remarkable achievements.

The 2000 U.S. Open at Pebble Beach proved an apt foreshadowing of the "Tiger Slam." Golf scribes had plenty of story lines to work with entering the event — namely, this would be Jack Nicklaus's final Open at one of golf's most spectacular venues. Tiger, however, decided to steal the show.

continued on next page

Woods put on a performance at Pebble that may never be seen again. He opened the week with a brilliant 65. By Sunday, he led by ten strokes. On some of the game's nastiest greens, Tiger didn't flinch. He didn't miss a putt within ten feet once in 72 holes. His final round 67 put him 12 under par for the tournament — 15 strokes in front of the runner-up. This was the greatest margin of victory for a major, and some say it was Tiger's best performance so far. Standing just off 18, Tiger offered this recap: "I felt very tranquil, very peaceful inside. And for some reason, no matter what happened out there, I was able to keep my cool and my composure and focus 100 percent on each and every shot."

A PRIZE FOR MIZE?

For Larry Mize, it was the ultimate dream come true. At the 1987 Masters Tournament, Mize was the local favorite. Born and raised just minutes from the course at Augusta National Golf Club, Mize had long dreamed of winning golf's most prestigious tournament, in what was virtually his own backyard. Though he had won only one tournament during his previous five-plus years on the Tour, Mize thought 1987 could be his year to win the big one.

"It was the biggest golfing thrill I think I could have," he recalls. "I was born and raised in Augusta, and as a youngster, I used to work the scoreboards — right there at the third green — for a couple of years. Going back there, it was a dream come true."

continued on next page

Mize was not considered a favorite by the experts when the week started, but by the time Sunday's final round came about, he was in the hunt. When all 72 holes of regulation had been completed, Mize was locked in a three-way tie with Greg Norman and Seve Ballesteros. Ballesteros had won the tournament in 1980 and 1983, and Norman had been in the hunt at Augusta before. In fact, at the time he was considered by some to be the world's best player. Mize, conversely, had just the one PGA tournament win to his credit, along with one runner-up finish. Still, he'd had a feeling about the 1986 Masters, even before the tournament began.

"I remember coming into town playing well, thinking I had a *chance* to win," he explains. "But I don't ever think you really count on winning. You think, 'I've got a chance to win.' You believe you can win; but really thinking it's actually going to happen, I don't think that comes to your mind. You just want to be there and have a chance. That's the way I felt.

"I played good all week and knew I had a chance [by] Saturday afternoon. I played three under from 13 on in, which really was the momentum that put me into Sunday and gave me some confidence for the last round. And I went out there Sunday thinking that I had a really good chance to win. I was a few shots back, nobody was paying any attention to me, and there were all the big names — Norman and Crenshaw and Seve and Bernhard Langer were up there. I was just going to try and just kind of slip in there. Sure enough, I took the lead when I birdied 12 and 13 — and gave it back on 14 and 15."

continued on next page

Mize almost saw his chance slip away at 18 but saved a birdie there to force the playoff. From there, it seemed the win was Mize's destiny. Ballesteros was eliminated at the first extra hole, and it came down to Mize and Norman. On the second playoff hole, things reached a dramatic end with what is perhaps the most memorable golf shot in history. With his ball resting 140 feet away from the pin, Mize calmly pulled out his sand wedge and chipped the ball into the hole to win the fabled green jacket. Few fans will ever forget the shot or the reaction from the normally laid-back Mize, who leaped into the air like he had been bounced from a trampoline.

"Once the shot went in the hole, it was just total excitement and disbelief that it went in," Mize recalls. "I think my jump and run says it all. I just couldn't believe it. I was totally elated. I remember going crazy. I mean, I started jumping up and down and running all around screaming. That's the funny thing. I was screaming.

"And then I realized, 'You're screaming. Be quiet.' Thank goodness we were far enough back where [I thought] people didn't hear me. But the network crew was there, and they said later, 'Oh yeah, we heard you yelling.' But that was just unbelief, in chipping it in, because I'm trying to hit a good shot and put the pressure back on Greg, but I wasn't expecting to chip it in. To chip it in to win the golf tournament was just incredible.

"To beat Greg and Seve was just icing on the cake — as was getting the jacket from Jack [Nicklaus], my childhood idol. It was just a tremendous week for me. The first thing I thought about after having won it was that I get to go back — I get to go back home to Augusta every April for the tournament."

THE BABE

Of all the great golfers over the years, by many accounts the most naturally gifted athlete the game has ever seen may well have been the one simply known as "Babe." Mildred "Babe" Didrikson, a 5-foot-5 woman from Port Arthur, TX, was one of the great athletes in American history. After making her mark at the Olympics, she became one of the most successful golfers of her era — male or female.

Growing up in rural Texas, Didrikson dominated basketball and track and field. She set world records in the javelin, high jump, hurdles, and the softball throw. She also swam and participated competitively in tennis, diving, boxing, volleyball, and skating. When asked if there was anything she didn't play, Babe replied, "Yeah, dolls."

In 1933, following her success at the 1932 Olympics — where she won two gold medals and one silver — Didrikson began looking for a new challenge. She turned to golf, a game that she had briefly encountered in high school. Before long, her natural talent took over, and by 1935, she had won the Texas Women's Amateur. In all, she won 55 tournaments, including three U.S. Women's Opens. This included an incredible stretch of 31 tournament wins in just five years. Perhaps her greatest contribution to golf was her role in founding the Ladies Professional Golf Association in 1949.

Didrikson's defining moment came in the wake of a battle with colon cancer. At age 43, just 14 months after major surgery, Didrikson won her third and final U.S. Open by an astounding 12 strokes. It was one of the most courageous feats in sports. "It just proved how tough she was and what a great competitor and abilities she had," said Byron Nelson.

"My goal was to be the greatest athlete who ever lived," Didrikson said of her accomplishments. By some accounts, she may very well have achieved that goal.

GREATEST GOLF SHOT

Every golfer longs for that one shot that will
define him or her. When experts are asked about
the greatest shot in golf history, most recall
Gene Sarazen's shot in the final round of the
1935 Masters.

Sitting three shots back of the clubhouse
leader, Sarazen stood atop a hill on the par 5
15th with a decision to make — a decision that
has plagued golfers throughout the ages:
Go for it, or lay up.

After a long drive off the tee, Sarazen faced
235 yards, over water, to the hole. Knowing
that he needed at least a birdie to remain in
contention, he decided to go for it. Sarazen
unleashed his 4-wood and connected perfectly
with the ball. The gallery watched as Sarazen's
ball soared safely over the water, onto the green,
and into the hole for an incredible double eagle.
Sarazen could hardly believe it as he scratched

out a two on his score card. Clubhouse leader Craig Wood, who was preparing to receive the tournament trophy, looked on in disbelief. He had watched his three-stroke lead disappear with one swing.

What followed was one of the greatest playoffs in Masters history. It is, in fact, the Masters' only 36-hole playoff, which Sarazen won by five shots. But what will forever be remembered about that day is Sarazen's double eagle at 15.

BEN THERE, DONE THAT

Ben Crenshaw has been a part of many memorable golf moments. None was more special than the 1995 Masters. Crenshaw spent the day before the tournament at the funeral of his coach, the beloved Harvey Penick. Crenshaw and his coach were particularly close, and the loss was devastating.

After briefly contemplating withdrawing from the tournament, Crenshaw decided to devote the week to his mentor, who loved the Masters. While his gesture was admirable, most golf experts had written Crenshaw off. His game wasn't in top form, and the loss of a loved one, they postulated, would shake even the most resilient athlete.

"I tried as hard as I could that week to think about what Harvey would tell me," said Crenshaw, "and that is, trust yourself and play simply — play by instinct. I somehow had a peace and calm and belief in myself that week."

That peace afforded Crenshaw the mindset needed to play beautifully. Using the technique that Penick helped him perfect, "Gentle Ben" did not record a single three-putt during the tournament. He shot a 14 under par and beat Davis Love III by one stroke. After sinking the winning putt, Crenshaw let loose the emotions that he had worked so hard to contain throughout the week. What followed was one of the most emotional moments that have ever been witnessed on a golf course. He buckled over on the green and wept.

"I'm totally convinced that I was put there for a reason that week," Crenshaw said afterward.

ABOVE PAR

MEMORABLE GOLF MOMENTS

HOGAN'S A HERO

Ben Hogan is one of golf's most revered figures. He is considered by many as the best ball striker ever. He captured 64 PGA Tour wins, including nine Majors. His success on the course was attributed to his seemingly flawless swing. For years, many have tried to learn what the key to that swing is. It has long simply been called "Hogan's Secret."

In a 1955 *Life* magazine article, several golf experts stated Hogan's secret was a special wrist movement known as "cupping under." *Golf Digest* later contended that the secret involved Hogan's right knee movement and how it mirrored the way he moved his wrist. Still, no one has uncovered the true basis of the secret.

Perhaps the real "secret" of Hogan's success is much simpler. Many golfers believe it was his astounding dedication to practice. Hogan spent countless hours at the driving range, working hard to perfect his swing until it appeared effortless.

Many times, Hogan would practice until his hands were bloody and swollen — and he was unable to properly grip his club. Legend has it that Hogan would then go and ice his hands until the blood coagulated and the swelling went down. Then he would practice some more.

The work ethic and determination that Hogan showed in his early years helped create what many consider his defining moment. In the winter of 1949, Hogan and his wife ran head-on into a school bus while traveling on a foggy Texas highway. They survived the accident, but Hogan suffered a broken pelvis, a fractured collarbone, a chipped rib, a fractured ankle, and dangerous blood clots. The clotting would create lifelong circulation problems. In fact, doctors once told Hogan he might never walk again, much less play professional golf.

continued on next page

Undeterred, Hogan worked tirelessly to recover, and just 16 months later, he entered the U.S. Open. While fans admired Hogan's determination, most considered him a nice story but certainly no contender.

Enduring excruciating pain, Hogan spent each night of the tournament soaking in a bathtub, trying to improve the blood flow in his legs. Playing with Ace bandages wrapped tightly around both legs, he finished regulation tied for the lead. An 18-hole playoff with Lloyd Mangrum and George Fazio ensued. But could Hogan complete another 18 holes in his condition?

Not only did Hogan finish, he won. A one under par 69 was enough to beat Mangrum by four strokes and Fazio by six. In storybook fashion, Hogan sealed the victory with a 50-foot birdie putt at 17.

While most thought he had no chance, Hogan still had a "secret." Hard work and determination gave him his most meaningful and amazing victory.

THE COMEBACK

In November 1991, Steve Jones crashed his dirt bike, spraining an ankle, separating a shoulder, and tearing ligaments in his left ring finger. Because of the damage to that one digit, that one small appendage, the career of one of golf's most promising young players was threatened. The injured finger would keep Jones off the PGA Tour for three years and force him to make a major change in his game. Most in the golf community thought he would never come back.

"At first I thought, 'Well, you know my finger's jammed a little bit and my shoulder hurts. I'll be back in a couple of months,'" recalls Jones. "Next thing I know, it was two and a half years before I could even swing a club. I didn't know if I was ever going to play golf again. Still, I didn't feel like my career was over. But it took me a year to get my swing going again."

continued on next page

Jones switched to a reverse-overlap grip to protect his finger, which would never be completely healed. At 30, the former up-and-coming star was forced to completely rebuild his game. Often he felt like giving up. But Jones knew he still had the passion to play golf — and that the talent was still there. Thousands of hours of rehabilitation and extra work finally paid off. In 1996, Jones won the U.S. Open at Bloomfield Hills, MI. Coming off his troubles, Jones was as unlikely an Open champion as golf had seen in years. "It was amazing to go from playing pretty well up through 1991, to all of a sudden not knowing if you're ever going to play again, to winning a Major," said Jones.

Tom Lehman, who played with Jones in the final round of the '96 Open and is one of his best friends, might have been the only person besides Jones' wife, Bonnie, who wasn't surprised. "People forgot how good a player he was before he got hurt," says Lehman. "When he won it [the Open] the attitude was, 'Where did this guy come from?' But Steve proved himself a long time ago. He deserves to win. He has the game to win."

Through his trials, Jones never felt sorry for himself, never caught himself asking "Why me?"

He notes, "A lot of people have said, 'Why do you think this happened to you?' And I said, 'Well, I know why it happened; I know why I got in a motorcycle wreck.' And they said, 'You do? Why?' My answer, 'Because I was a terrible rider."

"I might never have won a Major if I hadn't gotten injured. I definitely wouldn't have been as interesting doing interviews...You are going to have troubles in your life. You won't always have mountaintop experiences. The good times never last. The bad times never last. You do the best you can and move on."

THE HARD WORKING (AND UNSUNG) PRODIGY

In four years, Larry Nelson went from picking up a golf club for the first time to playing on the PGA Tour. Nelson grabbed a club for the first time at age 21. By age 25, he was playing against Jack Nicklaus and Tom Watson.

Nelson's formula for rapid success: innate athletic ability combined with a singular work ethic and self-discipline. Nelson's drive to improve was voracious. He attacked practice sessions and worked tirelessly at every facet of the game.

The work paid off. Sure, Nelson broke 100 the first time he played a regulation course but broke 70 less than nine months later. Less than four years after his first round of golf, he joined the Tour. In 1981, just 12 years after the first day he picked up a club, Nelson won a major tournament at the PGA Championship. The golf world was astonished, the experts speechless. Nelson remembers well the reaction from the press:

"Well, the first major championship I won was the PGA in Atlanta. It really meant a lot to me, because after you win a few tournaments, everybody says, 'Well, you know, he's not *really* a great player — or one of the top players — until he wins one of the Majors. So I won the PGA.

"So the next thing was, 'Well, you're not really a great player until you win two Majors.' So then I won the U. S. Open in 1983 and a couple of tournaments in between.

"Then they say, 'Well, yeah, a lot of people have won two Majors.' And then when I won the third (Major), for me there was a lot of self-satisfaction. But from the outside golfing world and the news media, it was kind of looked on as a fluke, simply because I did not have any amateur background playing in college. This was something that wasn't supposed to happen.

continued on next page

So it was pretty much dismissed by a lot of people. But I got a lot of great satisfaction out of that."

Nelson's wins at the U.S. Open in 1983 and the PGA Championship in 1981 and 1987 showed just what a talented player he had become. He stared down defending champ Tom Watson at the Open and beat him by one stroke in the last round. At the PGA, he ran away from Fuzzy Zoeller in '81, and out-dueled Lanny Wadkins in a playoff in '87. During the 1980s, Nelson joined Watson, Jack Nicklaus, and Seve Ballesteros as the only four players to win three or more Majors. Still, few in the golf circles even took notice of the elite company Nelson had joined.

"If you asked a trivia question of the four people who won at least three Majors in the 1980s," Nelson concedes, "people could probably come up with three of the four names. Mine would be the fourth. This is kind of a game sometimes that you have to be satisfied with your achievements. Somebody explained to me that success is being happy with what you have. So I feel like I'm very successful."

LET 'ER RIP

The date was April 7, 1935. The event was the second ever Masters tournament. During the final round, Gene Sarazen stood ready to hit his second shot on the 15th hole. Sarazen was a short, stocky man with massive forearms. He used a 15-ounce driver and sometimes swung the club so hard that he lost his balance. His overall playing style reflected his swing — he was always on the attack, always shooting for the flag.

On the 15th, Sarazen found himself more than 260 feet from the flag. He selected a 4-wood, stepped up, and hit the ball with authority. The ball flew to the pin and dropped into the cup. Sarazen's 2 on the par 5 hole tied him for the lead with Craig Wood, who ended up losing an 18-hole playoff by five strokes. Sarazen's big shot foreshadowed a legendary career — and a day when big hitters would rule the game.

THE PAUSE THAT REFRESHES

Gene Sarazen steadfastly claimed that his amazing double-eagle 2 on the 15th hole at Augusta National in 1935 was not the greatest shot of his life. In his view, his best shot came during the 1931 Ryder Cup match at Scioto Country Club in Columbus, OH. Facing off against Fred Robson, Sarazen whacked a tee shot over the green and into a refreshment stand. "I found my ball in the middle of the stand in a crevice in the concrete," Sarazen recalled. "No free drops back then. A window toward the green was open, so I played the ball through the window and onto the green about eight feet from the hole. That was the greatest shot. Robson three-putted and I sank my putt to win the hole," he noted proudly.

FOUR ACES WITH FOUR ACES

In one of the most amazing feats in golf history, four players aced the same hole during the same round of the 1989 U.S. Open. Mark Wiebe, Jerry Pate, Nick Price, and Doug Weaver all used 7-irons to knock their tee shots into the cup on the 167-yard 6th hole at Oak Hill Country Club in Rochester, N.Y.

The odds against such a feat? 8,675,083 to 1.

YOU WERE SAYING...

At the 1954 U.S. Open, members of Baltusrol Golf Club complained that Robert Trent Jones, the course designer, had made the par 3, 194-yard 4th hole too demanding. So Jones, accompanied by the club pro and club president, went out to the 4th tee, teed up a ball, and proceeded to knock the ball into the cup for a hole in one. Then he turned to the two men with him and said, "As you can see, the hole really isn't too difficult."

NEVER TOO FAR BACK

Arnold Palmer was in serious trouble as he entered the final round of the 1960 U.S. Open at Cherry Hills. He was seven strokes from the lead with 14 golfers ahead of him. It seemed there was no chance he could pull out a victory. Yet Arnie was convinced otherwise.

He stepped up to the first tee to begin the final round. The hole was 346 yards from tee to green. Palmer crushed his tee shot. With the gallery looking on in amazement, the ball flew onto the green. With this tee shot, Palmer kicked off what Herbert Warren Wind called "the most explosive stretch of sub-par golf any golfer has ever produced."

Palmer shot a 30 on the front nine. By hole 10, he had made up the seven strokes, climbed over the 14 people ahead of him, and grabbed a share of the lead. By the 12th hole, the lead was his alone. Palmer shot a 65 that day and captured his first U.S. Open title — all because he refused to believe he was too far back to have a chance.

19TH HOLE

INSPIRATION & HEROICS
ON & OFF THE COURSE

ON THE BALL

Golfers are some of the most superstitious athletes on the planet. From the weekend hacker to the Tour pro, most players follow a specific routine before each season, tournament, and even swing.

After experiencing a devastating loss as a result of a rookie mistake, Tour veteran Pat Bates began his own golf ritual.

Late in the 1993 season, Bates was looking for a victory on the Canadian Tour. He was in third place going into the tenth hole on the event's final round — in perfect position to make a run at the lead. However, an errant second shot on a long par 5 disappeared beyond the fairway.

Golfers are required to find lost balls within five minutes, or they are forced to take a drop and a penalty stroke. With the clock ticking, Bates searched frantically.

"I looked and looked around for that ball but couldn't find it," he recalls.

Just before time expired, Bates found a lonely Titleist buried in the rough. He managed to escape the hole with what appeared to be a bogey 6. The true test, however, began after Bates had sunk his five-foot putt.

"When I pulled the ball out of the cup, I realized that it was an old Titleist 5, all nicked and cut up. I realized, 'Oh my gosh — this is not my ball!' What were the chances of my finding another Titleist 5 in there?"

Risking a potential victory and prize money, Bates decided to do the honorable thing and report his mistake to the scorekeeper.

Says Bates, "I went to the scorer, thinking I was disqualified. But he said it was only a two-shot penalty for hitting the wrong ball, plus having to go back to the place where the ball was hit. So I ended up with a ten."

continued on next page

Still, the error was costly. Bates was pushed out of contention and lost thousands of dollars.

Since that experience, however, Pat Bates has taken extreme measures to avoid a similar mistake.

"I'd done the same thing ["found" the wrong ball] once before in college, and I thought, 'This is crazy.' I needed to mark my ball; there's no doubt about that. So I opened up my Bible that night and realized I needed to start marking my balls with Bible verses."

Bates' system has proved to be more inspirational than a simple dot or his initials.

"At one point in 1994," he explains, "I flew to three straight tournaments, including a Monday through Wednesday tournament. For those tournaments I wrote Hebrews 10:36: "For you have need of endurance, so that after you have done the will of God, you may receive the promise." That was to give me endurance for a couple of weeks — and it worked! I finished second, second, and eighth in those three tournaments!"

A LOVE STORY

Golf is not always a link between fathers and sons, but it certainly was for the Davis Loves. This was true from the start. In 1964, Davis Love Jr., a sometime touring pro who had played golf for Harvey Penick at the University of Texas, competed in the Masters Tournament. (In fact, he led the field after the first round.) The day after the tournament ended, Davis III was born.

Davis Jr. went on to establish himself as an outstanding teacher, first at Charlotte Country Club, then at Atlanta Country Club, and eventually at the *Golf Digest* teaching facility at the Cloister on Sea Island, GA. He taught his pupils in the simple, easily digestible style of his mentor, Penick, who was like a second father to him. Davis Jr.'s style changed when it came to his son, who became his most famous pupil.

continued on next page

Davis Jr.'s expectations for his son were high, and his son absorbed those desires and made them his own. Ironically, the most significant thing lacking in the father's game — length off the tee — was one of the son's most conspicuous blessings. For Davis Jr., teaching his son golf was his clearest way of being a father; Davis III, called "Trip" for his numeral, came to recognize the lessons as expressions of his father's love. They weren't just father and son, teacher and pupil; they were also best friends and partners in the enterprise of young Davis's career.

In his first three years on Tour, Davis Love III established himself as an outstanding talent, with a win in Hilton Head and over half a million dollars in earnings. But the father felt his son was stagnating — his third season had been particularly disappointing. Shortly before Davis III was to travel to Hawaii for the Kapalua Invitational in November 1988, his father asked him to go for a ride, during which he delicately broached the subject of Trip's working with another teacher. "I'm wondering if I've taken you as far as you can go," the father confided.

"I just wonder if there isn't somebody else who could take you to the next level." Davis III was shocked and also adamant that he wanted to continue working under his father's eye. He promised to increase his dedication to his practice regimen, and he flew to Hawaii feeling invigorated.

While Davis III was in Hawaii, he ran into a pastor, an old friend of his parents'. He called home to check in and tell his folks about seeing their friend. His mother, Penta, told Davis that his father and one of his teaching associates, Jimmy Hodges, had taken a charter flight from Sea Island to Jacksonville, en route to a seminar in Tampa. Unfortunately, their plane had disappeared from the radar. Davis caught a flight from Hawaii to San Francisco, not knowing yet if his father was dead or alive. By the time Davis arrived in San Francisco and found a pay phone, the small plane had been found. There were no survivors.

continued on next page

Davis was devastated. He had lost the most important person in his life. For months after the crash, Davis would wake up sobbing uncontrollably. By his own admission, he went through the next year and a half in a daze. His talent assured him of a good living playing on Tour, but he wasn't improving, and time was slipping away. In May 1990, while playing in a tournament in Japan, he had a bracing talk with teaching pro Butch Harmon, who knows a thing or two about the influence of a strong father — his was also a legendary teacher who won the 1948 Masters. The talk woke Davis out of his torpor; he finished third that weekend, and three months later, he won his second Tour event.

In 1991, Davis won at Hilton Head again and finished eighth on the money list. Then, in 1992, in the tournament often referred to as the "fifth Major" — the Players Championship — Davis won his biggest title yet on the Sawgrass course that lies just a few miles from the site where his father's plane crashed. Starting the final day three strokes behind Nick Faldo, he shot the day's low round of 67 on his way to

a four-shot victory. The final round was played
under gray skies, but as Davis putted on the
final green, the sun peeked through the clouds,
and in no time, it was a bright and shining day.
Robin Love, his wife, told him on that final
green, "That's your dad, shining down at you
in your moment of glory."

The years went by, and Davis continued
to rank among the world's top players, but he
increasingly found himself saddled with the title
"Best Player Never to Have Won a Major." Some
questioned his killer instinct; he was one and
five in playoffs, and while his demeanor on the
course was formal, perhaps even a little stiff, his
fellow professionals knew him as someone who
might be too nice to be a world beater.

As 1996 wound down, Davis collaborated
on a book describing the lessons he'd learned
from his father. The title, *Every Shot I Take*,
reflected how often Davis thought about his
father's influence. He would later say that the
process of putting his father's thoughts and

continued on next page

teachings between hard covers — and of talking at length about his father's death, something that he, his mother, his brother, and his wife all did for the book — helped him view that tragedy from a different perspective, helped him recognize how time had passed and that he was ready for a kind of healing, a kind of acceptance that had eluded him.

In 1997, Davis's best finish in the year's first three Majors was third place at the Masters, where he finished four strokes behind Tom Kite in the Merely Human Flight (Tiger Woods was an otherworldly twelve strokes ahead of Kite). But at Winged Foot for the PGA Championship, he tied for the first-round lead with a 66, adding another 66 on Saturday. He entered the final round tied for the lead with Justin Leonard; the two would play in the last Sunday pairing. After nine holes, Davis had opened up a five-stroke lead.

On the par 5 12th, however, Leonard birdied while Love bogeyed, and on the 13th hole Love hit his worst shot of the day, pulling the ball into long rough on the short side left of the green. Meanwhile, Leonard put his shot 15 feet from the cup. But Davis hit a lob wedge that nearly went in, then made the 2-foot putt to keep the lead at three.

Rains poured throughout the last nine holes, but as Davis drove from the final tee with a four-shot lead, the skies began to brighten. As he walked up to the final green, the sun came through once again, just as it had at Sawgrass five years earlier. Only this time, there wasn't just sunshine, there was also a rainbow, framed by CBS's cameras in a view that ran it directly from the sky down to the hole as Davis approached his final putt. Rolling the 12-foot birdie putt home, he then embraced first his friend Justin Leonard; then his brother and caddie, Mark; then his wife, Robin; and finally his mother, Penta. "Dad knows what you've done," she told him.

"I know," he replied.

A love story was requited at last.

QUITTING, TO WIN

In 1986, Laurie Brower, then a Southern California junior golf champ and two-time Southwest Conference Player of the Year at Texas Tech, decided to try the LPGA's qualifying school. She felt ready to contend for a spot on the Pro Tour.

She was on her way to making the Tour when she tore the cartilage in her wrist while hitting a routine fairway shot. Her wrist became so sore that she couldn't pick up a pencil. X-rays showed the bones in her wrist had fused together. Following surgery, one doctor told Laurie she would never play golf again.

Brower spent 18 months rehabilitating the wrist before she was ready to give the Tour another shot. On the eve of making her comeback attempt, she received an urgent telephone call from her father. He told Laurie her mother was dying of a brain tumor.

Brower had waited a year and a half for the opportunity to prove she could play with the best golfers in the world. She had recovered from the wrist injury. It was her time to shine. Yet when her dad called, there was no hesitation as to what she would do. "My dad asked me to quit work. I did," Brower said. "I never asked why. It was my mother."

For two and a half years, Brower put golf aside and took care of her mother. There were good and bad days. On good days, her mom was normal, could hold a conversation, and remembered what life once was. Other days were far worse.

continued on next page

"When she woke up from naps, she would scream with fear if nobody was there," Brower said. "So I tried to stay close by. I was there whenever anything bad happened."

Brower knew she was losing the best years of her golf career, but she didn't care. Her mom was more important. Her only practice came in the backyard of her parents' home, hitting balls into a net and putting on a small patch of Astro Turf. "I was very thankful for that time with my mom," Brower said. "Being home with her, I got to spend so much quality time. I wouldn't change any of it. None of it. I had to watch her deteriorate, but...I was there for her."

Dorothy Brower died in 1989. Shortly thereafter, Laura Brower got a call from a friend asking her to play in a mini-tour event in Southern California. Brower initially said no. She still wasn't emotionally ready. After some persuading, she agreed to play.

As she stepped up to the first tee, she realized
it was the same course where her mom had last
watched her play. Emotion overwhelmed her.
She shot a 9 on the 1st hole. She doubted her
ability to finish, but then she "realized my mom
wouldn't want to see me like this."

Brower rallied to shoot a 75, finished fifth,
and earned $900. "It was time to get the ball
rolling," she decided. Less than a year later, in
October 1991, she made the LPGA Tour.
It was five years later than scheduled, but
Brower was much more fulfilled because of
all she had endured.

A PLAYER'S PLAYER

Gary Player is one of the most celebrated golfers in the world. The native of South Africa is the only player to win the British Open in three different decades — claiming the title in 1959, 1968, and 1974. In all, he has won 21 tournaments on the PGA Tour, including victories in each of the four Majors. Along with his triumphs at the British, he won the PGA Championship in 1962 and 1972, the U.S. Open in 1965, and the Masters in 1961 and 1974 — becoming the third golfer ever to win the coveted "grand slam."

Player is also known as one of the kindest and friendliest men to play on the Tour. The diminutive athlete had to overcome childhood heartache to become the man he is today. "I lost my mother, when I was eight years of age, from cancer," Player recalls. "My father was working in the gold mines in South Africa, 14,000 feet underground. My brother was fighting in the last world war alongside the Americans. I was alone most of the time in my youth."

But rather than become bitter over his struggles, Player chose to become thankful for all he had. That heart of gratitude still exists today, as Player is keenly aware of how much he has been blessed. "It's very difficult when a young boy loses his mother at that age," Player says. "But then you look around and you see some children who don't have any parents. There's always somebody worse off than you are. "

Player's experience with tragedy has not only given him perspective on his own life but has also inspired him to use his personal pain as motivation to reach out to others in need. He constantly searches for ways he can make a difference in the lives of others. "I think being on my own and being so lonely, it just really makes me very sad when I think of so many children that are left alone," Player explains. "They don't have education, don't have a home — and don't have food or clothing. This kind of thing happened to me, so I can relate to it. And if I can help in any way, that's one of my big dreams."

continued on next page

Help he has. Through an outreach program based at his home, Player makes a daily impact on the lives of South African youth — helping to secure their futures. "We have this magnificent school on my farm in South Africa for 400 students," says Player. "We feed them twice a day. I'm having people come along and help me — whether it's providing pencils or footballs or books or any kind of assistance. People have been very kind. The joy that it's given me, it's like winning the Masters tournament, seeing the joy on the children's faces.

"We all try to leave the earth a little bit better place than what we found it," he says, "whether it's planting a tree, being kind to an old lady, winning a golf championship, or visiting children in a hospital. Whatever the case may be — we've got to try and leave it a better place."

DALY DEVOTION

Golfer John Daly often makes news for his antics away from the golf course, so stories like the one below sometimes get lost amid the tabloid fodder.

At the 1991 PGA Championship, a then unknown Daly drove through the night from Memphis to the Crooked Stick Golf Club in Carmel, IN, where he had earned the last position in the tournament. He arrived on the scene so late that he didn't have time to play a practice round or even look at the course. But the sleep-deprived, road-weary Daly found a way to win the tournament. Sadly, the event was marred by a lightning strike that claimed the life of a gallery patron. Daly donated $30,000 of his winnings, his first significant check as a professional, to the victim's family.

GREAT SAVE

In 1988, LPGA player Mary Beth Porter was playing to qualify for the Standard Register Turquoise Classic when she heard a small child calling for help. Porter saw that a three-year-old boy, Jonathan Smucker, was drowning in his family's pool in a nearby yard. She vaulted a seven-foot fence, pulled the boy from the pool, and administered CPR until paramedics arrived. Jonathan made a full recovery. Back on the course, Porter failed to shoot low enough to qualify after resuming her round, but the LPGA commissioner gave her a special exemption to play the remainder of the tournament.

WHAT A COMEBACK!

Judy Eller Street was a junior at the University of Miami in 1959 when she won the national golf championship for women. Then, like many female golfers and athletes of that time, she dropped out of school to marry and start a family.

What's unusual is the way she dropped back in to school. In the mid-1990s, after her marriage broke up, Street decided to go back to college at Barry University in Miami Shores, FL. While attending a school banquet, the women's basketball coach, Jan Allen, heard Judy's story and her background. "Wouldn't it be funny," Allen told school officials, "if Judy had another year's eligibility and could play golf here?" Intrigued, the officials did some checking and discovered that Street indeed had one more year of eligibility. So at the age of 62, Judy Street became the number-three player on the golf team, helping Barry reach sixth in the NCAA Division 2 rankings — and making Judy the oldest NCAA athlete on record.

If you have enjoyed this book,
Hallmark would love to hear from you.
Please send your comments to

BOOK FEEDBACK
HALLMARK CARDS, INC.
2501 MCGEE, MAIL DROP 215
KANSAS CITY, MO 64141-6580

Or email us at booknotes@hallmark.com